BOND WITH REALITY OF LIFE

SUKHMANPREET KAUR

Contents

Contents

Contents

Introduction

This book is not going to reveal any secrets of the life; it is going to remind you about the life. The happiness and the gratitude that you forget to showcase to yourselves, it will be a reminder for you. How we act and what we think are both stated in the book. The confrontation of hard times is crucial to succeeding; this fact will be highlighted by the book. Consistency, self-talk, and completion are the focal points. To make ourselves organized with hard work is a necessity but putting hard work in the right direction is the focus. Our determination ought to be determined for the goals. With all the catastrophes you have faced, you are facing, or you will face, admitting defeat should not enter in our minds. The thoughts of inspiration and appreciation for life should remain alive in our hearts, souls, and minds. This is what the book is going to refresh in your memory.

Inspire, and just be inspired,

Determine, and just be determined,

Achieve and be unbeatable,

Happy and just be happy.

Actually, this is something that life wants to make us realise all the time.

Adore life and enjoy reading.

CHAPTER ONE

FOLLOW WHAT YOU LIKE

*"Do what you want to that do,
Do not do that which is liked by others."*

Everyone is performing a different profession, but some don't like a lot. It is because they are following a profession, which is not liked by them. The thing which you like, you will see a massive increment in that because that is what you like to do. Let's try to understand this with a graph.

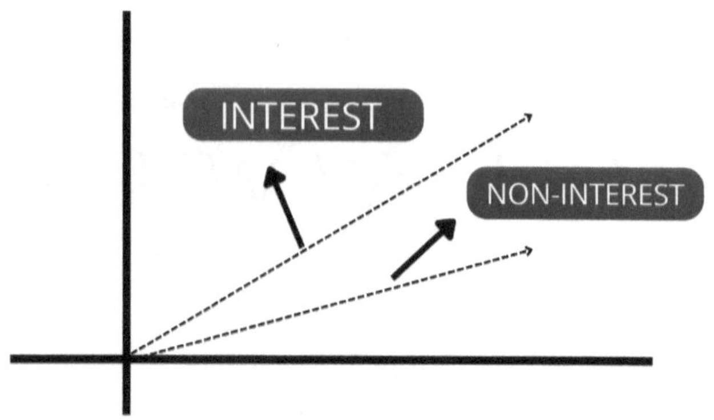

FIGURE - 1

GRAPH OF INTEREST AND NON-INTEREST

In the above graph, it's clearly visible that the more interest we have, the more progress we will get.

Now you will have a question,

Do we need to quit what we are doing and have to find interest?

The answer to this is clearly "NO". If you are not getting satisfaction from your job, then try to find INTEREST in that, rather than quitting it. When you find even a bit of interest in your profession, you will automatically try to be a professional in that and that is what you are trying to have for a long ago.

Another thing, which you can attempt is to manage your time to find interest. Even if you do not have the skill, it's okay to learn that skill and if you say, you don't have time, then there are some points which one can follow:

1. Just do some research about it.

2. Prepare a proper road map.
3. Learn the skill, even for 30 minutes a day. {Set time according to your planner}

If you believe it's less time, then think 30 minutes per day, it will be a greater amount in long run.

Per day⇒30 minutes

Per week⇒3.5 hours

Per month⇒14 hours

If another thought you have about your hectic schedule, then remember:

"Being tired is the symbol of hard work.

Your tiredness measures your hard work level".

Doing it consistently will help in the long run.

"Our future depends on our actions.

Because our actions decide what we will make in the future".

Conclusion: -

Simply, we can say that

1. Interest rate is directly proportional to success rate.

The more interest you will develop, more success will generate.

1. Do actions consistently.
2. Learn the skill, even for 30 minutes a day. {Set time according to your planner}

CHAPTER TWO

ACTIONS MATTER

We all want to have a luxurious life, want to enjoy a deluxe lifestyle, enjoying different suites, we all are passionate about it. But here the question which arises is:

The actions we perform for that Is it enough for that?

The answer to this question is only known to you, one knows his / herself better, it doesn't matter how much any other person knows you. Well, to have the best, we have to do better daily. The others thinking shouldn't affect you, only this simple thing you have to be mindful of and your flawless hard work will give you desirable results. Now, what to do, to do better daily?

There are some points that you all should be mindful of:

- Keep off Insanity - You can't expect different results by performing the same work. But yes, revising over and over is the exceptional case here.

- Block your time →You must note here that, you have to block time for specific hours, it will work differently for everyone.

In the case of a student, it will work like this:

TIME SHOULD BE ACCORDING TO YOU

STUDY SESSION-1	**2 hours**
STUDY SESSION-2	**3 hours**
STUDY SESSION-3	**1 hour**
STUDY SESSION-4	**2 hours**

FIGURE - 2

In the case of an office person, it will be kind of this:
- Morning rituals
- Office timings
- Back to home
- Bit hour of learning {that's action timing}

Apparently, remember your time blocking should be flexible and totally realistic.

The process you are following, it is just like your healthy meal, which is beneficial to you.

CHAPTER THREE

AN AMATEUR

Learning can never be bounded by age limits. Grasping knowledge starts with our birth and lasts up to our death. Every day new opportunity teaches us. People are afraid to be revealed as amateurs, but being an amateur is something, which I'm truly proud of.

An amateur knows how to fill the voids. How? To understand it better let's dive into another wave: -

The foremost question is who is an amateur?

Who works for the spirit of obsession, regardless of money, money will be automatically generated when you get obsessed with your work.

An amateur person is always passionate about learning, it always craves for grasping knowledge. They are well known to this fact that: -

"Doing something is better than doing nothing.

Even a stupid act can be helpful."

Even sharing some of your work online at regular intervals of time, is quite an effective way to showcase what you are, obviously, you are learning, but it is not bad to share. It's the modern age, it's not the time of the medieval age, where one day, bulb light strikes in your head and one is going to escape for long years in a cabin and try to make a single product for years.

BENEFIT OF BEEN AN AMATEUR

No-one is perfect in everything. So, been an amateur it's not a typical thing to learn anything. So, enjoy in doing your process.

One's life should be defined according to his/her definition of life. Enjoy your life on your own terms.

Best way to learn from others:

While sharing your work online (either skill you have learnt or you are learning) you can lookout for the people who are interested in this work, just surf. If they are sharing just have a look what they are sharing, try to fill your gaps through them and gradually try to take note on voids, which you can fill. And that's how we can learn.

Apparently, one can gain the perfection through being an amateur. In the beginning be an amateur, like you don't know anything, but at the end be a proficient in the field. That's the real meaning of AMATEUR.

CHAPTER FOUR

COURAGE

"Solve the troubles with courage and then move forward on your path."

"We always think that only not me, you, and you all, the very same thing. Why do problems come into our life? We all have a misconception if we don't have any issues in our life, so life becomes very easeful. But remember problems tell us, what is life."

We need to understand we can't resist hard time in our life. It's okay to have a hard time. It will teach you better, don't try to be so harsh on yourself, during this interval of time. We can understand our capability of handling situations and on top of that, "HOW WE HANDLE OURSELVES?"

"In problems and depression always remember, God's gifts are precious, we all are the creatures of God, how we can forget ourselves?"

In case you are trying to be so hard on yourself, don't do that. Some simple tips, although effective all the time are listed below:

1. To calm yourself have a conversation with nature.

2. Talk with yourself. Does it sound crazy? but it's quite an authentic way to calm ourselves. Using this:

- You will be able to figure out the situation more clearly.
- Self-talk helps to have better solutions.

There are another three points which can be followed:

1. Meditate→ This is the method we hear from thousands but only a few implicate it and those who do that, they are known to the results.
2. Keep off losing the strength.
3. - Keep off changing the path due to obstacles.

"Problems can make you weak, at that instant, but in fact, only problems make us strong."

CHAPTER FIVE

OUR TRADEMARK

"Thoughts of person's mind show person's personality."

Our day-to-day engagements with others, always leave our trademark on them. People get to know about us, how we treat them. However, the question is: Is our behavior determines our thinking? If yes, then how it depends on it?

Let's have a deep sight view of this.

Our behavior is directly or indirectly depending on our thoughts and our thoughts get affected by our emotions' state at that interval of time.

As mentioned above it's clear that how we act is the determining factor for our thinking.

If one doesn't want to leave a bad impression that person has to learn to control emotions. Although they affect indirectly however, they affect. This is another learning that boosts the confidence rate.

If the state of emotion is elated, without a doubt, people will have more interest to talk to you, and people would like to get inspired by you.

While having a conversation in depressed or livid mode, the graph of inspiration will be cut off indisputably.

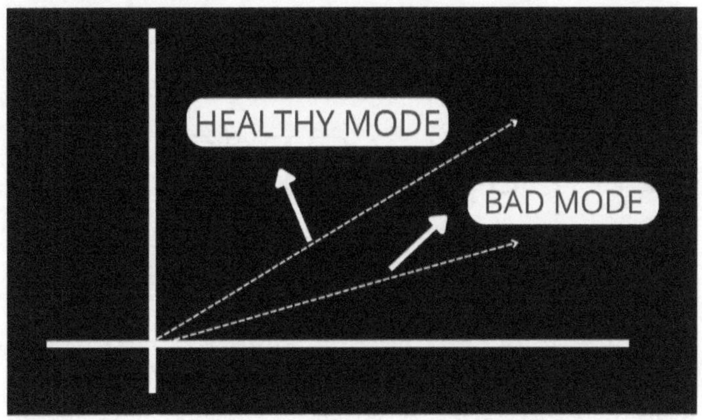

Enter Caption

From the above graph, we can simply conclude this fact that:

We should learn to control our emotions. So that we can have a command over our thoughts and when thoughts are under control, the conversation will be inspired full.

CHAPTER SIX

MEANING OF SUCCESS

Everyone has a different meaning of success. People define it on their own terms. It is right to explain something on its own basis, having a different and unique definition. However, we try to come across with others' definition of life. It is good to listen to what is good, even implicate it. Apparently, we try to focus on other things daily. The majority follow this same rule. Mostly, that is the reason only a few people can achieve high things. But

What is success for you?

Do you think that success means "TO ACHIEVE SOMETHING BIGGER?"

As mentioned earlier, it is different for everyone. Does that mean we all have to adopt a distinct strategy for our pathway? The answer is exactly "YES."

You might be wondering what success means to me?

The journey from the day until the end of the night, whatever I have learnt in that interval of time, that is what success means to me.

While performing daily activities, whatever mistakes I make, their learning is still a success to me. I am pleased to learn whatever I have learnt.

Now, it's time for a question: "HOW CAN ONE SPECIFY THEMSELVES?"

1. Recognize your weak points.

2. Recognize your areas of strength.

3. Design the plan based on your preferences.

4.Acting on that action plan.

5. Reviewing.

6. Learning.

This is one of the most widely used method. Even though it's widely used and most common, only a few can grasp this plan till the end. Apparently, anyone who survives in extreme conditions, it will live happily.

CHAPTER SEVEN

LEARNING PERIOD

Consider yourself a fish out of water, feeling anxious about something. Think about a situation where you felt the most anxious. If something truly bad happened to you, you wouldn't even want to recall that moment. You might consider that moment your worst moment. But why am I saying it?

We all come across situation where we have to face off a huge downfall. That's something we don't like, but apparently, it is a universal fact. Everyone has to face a drastic downfall, even if it is for a single time. But that plays a crucial role in enjoying luxurious suites. That moment becomes even more important because this is called the "LEARNING PERIOD."

What you have learnt in that phase is listed below.

- Gained confidence.

- You are the only best friend of yours.

- Except your parents, no one was there to give you back.

- Difference between trustworthy and non-reliable.

- Having a strong command of communication skills.

- Jurisdiction over emotions.
- Skills improvement.

These are the couple of skills that every person who has faced hard times has learnt.

Now, another question arises: HOW TO GET OVER THE ANXIETY? Again, there are not many unknown things you will know. These are already known to you, but the main thing to be noted here is that "YOU DO NOT IMPLICATE IT."

1. Take some time off.
2. Try to stay courageous.
3. Don't let yourself be affected by others.

If one practices these three listed points, one will gain the confidence to fight back against the anxiety.

CHAPTER EIGHT

COMPARISON

In this segment, let's compare something. Now you must be thinking, is it about comparing with any other person? Obviously, you all know this fact that we shouldn't compare ourselves to others, we must compare ourselves with ourselves. "HOW MUCH IS IT TRUE?"

Consider yourself a businessman who has been in this field for a long time. In the past few years, you have made remarkable progress. Your company has given unbeatable competition to other companies, but this time your company is in the downfall phase. To save a company from hard times, at that moment, what will you do?

There are two scenarios at present:

Case 1: Comparing your analytics with other companies' analytics.

Case 2: Comparing your analytics with your past years' progress data.

Which will you choose? Let's think about it and let's try to move deeper into it.

Some will choose case 1 and others will choose case 2. Right? Is there any alternative here? If I considered myself at that moment, I would choose both. What should I be doing?

So, I would compare my data with my own company's past progression data.

I will be discussing three listed below questions:

1) What were the points I have missed to make progress?

2) What's the change I did this year?

3) What blunders have I made?

These three are going to be the base questions which I'll discuss with myself and with my teammates.

That's how I'll use the case – 1

Now it's time to use case 2.

1) What do other companies are doing?

2) Contrasting my errors with their marketing strategy.

So, meanwhile, my strategy will be following both cases. Is that mean we have to follow both? Well, it depends upon the situation, but the most effective way is to compare the two cases. Because that will be the most profitable way.

Concluding it in a simple manner:

Comparing isn't a bad thing; how we implicate it matters. Comparing should be in a positive manner. We can not take it in a negative sense. We will be understanding positive and negative comparisons in further detail.

CHAPTER NINE

COMPARISON TYPES

In this context, let's segregate COMPARISON into two categories:

1. Positive comparison
2. Negative comparison

To understand this, let's consider a case:

Student – A who has been excelling in his or her class and a newly admitted student – B has taken first place. Student – A having an emotional breakdown. But, to return to his/her rank, what will that do now? Obviously, you are going to say:

- Hard-work
- Finding mistakes.
- Keeping off silly mistakes.
- Change in strategy.

These are some obvious tasks, which one is going to follow. But we forget something. Sometimes frustration occurs, when it seems like an unapproachable task. This frustration often become the cause of "COMPARISON."

And as earlier discussed, it can cause negative comparison.

Another question:

Which one is better? Before going to their differences, let's give a look at their definitions.

When we take comparison in a positive manner, it will be considered a positive comparison.

Similarly, whenever a comparison seems to be in a negative sense, it will be considered a negative comparison.

With the example of a student, if that student tries to find out their mistakes and takes a little bit of negative contrast, it will be useful. But how much negative sense will help? Just by understanding what's different that another student has done? That's not even negative a lot, although we are contrasting. So, I would say, in a positive and a little bit negative way, that will work out to get better results.

CHAPTER TEN

UNWRAPPING OF HAPPINESS

We all experience difficulties. We have dreadful anxiety for a couple of reasons. But we think why God always does this to me. We all know this fact that everyone has a hard time. No-one is always elated, but it is just that we feel only we have issues. There is always a fear in our head. It could be of darkness, height, or anything else. We all just try to escape from this fear. However, remember there are certain things which will give you happiness, what I call the "UNWRAPPING OF HAPPINESS."

Our happiness is just like a package that just needs to be unwrapped. There are irrefutable rules to accomplish this. Why am I saying so? The simplest reason behind this is that only a few people can break down the shell of "UNWRAPPING OF HAPPINESS."

Now, what are those certain things?

These are listed below.

UNWRAPPING OF HAPPINESS:

- Never feel you are a failure.
- Enjoy the small moments of life.

- Overcoming fear is the biggest happiness, so always do something that helps to overcome fear.

-Never blame yourself (if you don't lie)

Again, these are rules that are already known to you, but the difference you must generate now is to "IMPLICATE." When one starts implementing these rules, one will see a difference.

"No one is born with happiness, but successful persons live with a goal of accomplishment to create happiness."

"No one is born with happiness, but they are born with the accomplishment to create happiness."

Which things make you feel elated? Multiple reasons are there. But have you ever felt overwhelmed without reason?

Mostly, people say "NO." That's the mistake, and naturally, that's what resists you to breaking the case of "UNWRAPPING OF HAPPINESS."

CHAPTER ELEVEN

THOUGHTS

" "Abandon your bad thoughts (because life is yours) once you replace your bad thoughts with good ones, you make a successful step towards your journey." "

What better explains our destination?

The successful moves that we make daily – as success for me – is the enrichment of new learning every day. The steps we will take to have a productive day, those will make our day. Not a single word can explain what makes our destination better.

It will consist of some base terms, obviously, like

- Hard work
- A perfect strategy
- Daily accomplishment of goals
- Consistency
- Learning from mistakes

But one thing that one should be mindful of is *that we can't let negative and bad thoughts level up more than our positive ones.* We must keep the negative thoughts far away from us. When one can't achieve something for which one conspires, it leaves bad thoughts. There are multiple misperceptions that spring to mind. However, one needs to be careful because these considerations will only demotivate us. There will be no fruitful result, one will gain.

Through demotivating thoughts:

- One may feel that person is not capable of doing anything.
- The major misconception that we have, is that our capabilities are less than we think.
- We are not enough to do it.
- Others are better.

To avoid these thoughts, we need to keep on upgrade ourselves with our thoughts.

Even our technology demands upgrades. We want to have upgraded versions of mobile phones. Not just that, we want to improve every technology gadget. If change and upgrading are the necessities of life, then why can't we boost ourselves up and suppress our dim view.

CHAPTER TWELVE

SUKHMAN 4P RULE

The leading interrogation is "What is the 4 P Rule?" And what does "4 P" stand for?

The "4 P" stand for PREPARATION, PRODUCTIVITY, PROFICIENCY, and PROCRASTINATION.

What's it? Let's have a deeper look at it.

"Preparation is needed for every task; it doesn't matter whether it is for our good life or for our worse life because hard work is for the good life, and procrastination is also another type of preparation that helps in getting a worse life."

What we will be in our future, it's all going to depend on us. What we do determines what we get. Our preparation is much needed. Preparation and procrastination both create huge differences in one's life. If we do preparation consistently, it will enhance our productivity. On the contrary, if we are getting procrastinated consistently, will that help in our enhancement? Without doubt, the answer is "not by any means." But we all get procrastinated straightforwardly. The distractions make us dither. Whatever the fine ideas springing to mind, we are unable to scribble them down. We know this; however, we are unable to keep off distractions. "What one can do?"

It's not as easy as ABC to just avoid it. We all live in a modern world where everyone is connected to others through social media. We like to post our media onto social networking sites, but usage become the reason of distraction all the time. How to fix it? If we want to get benefits from there,

- The one thing that is suitable is to exchange your creative ideas and learn there. It will also not seem to be a distraction.
- Bound time: The most effective way one can go about it is to set themselves a time limit.

These two things can be done to resist procrastination.

To enrich the preparation, enhance productivity, and increase proficiency, decrease procrastination.

Vigorous and consistent productive days are directly proportional to good preparation, and similarly, procrastination is inversely proportional to the remaining 3P.

CHAPTER THIRTEEN

CYCLE OF FRUSTRATION AND WE

""Planners can be made so easily, the biggest obstacle in your planner is you, who are not following it effectively and are not considering it seriously.""

We all got obsessed with 2-3-minute motivational videos, which last up to minimum for some hours of the day and max to max for 2-3 days. Let's try to understand what we do in depth:

We get distracted easily for various reasons; the attraction of social networking sites becomes greater than our goal. This attractive force is pushing us to get distracted. And, when we looked at the time, we ended up wasting hours in scrolling. This becomes the reason of rise in frustration levels. We feel demotivated and end up wasting the whole day. This cycle can be considered a "CYCLE OF FRUSTRATION." Then, we just try to give motivation to ourselves by watching motivational videos, having a look at planning videos, and collecting tone of visual data. I'm not against watching videos; it's just when we feel exhausted and have no power to resume the work. At that point of time, one can surely go for that; it helps in boost us up.

When we collect the information, figure out some plans, and have the motivation to do it for at least some hours or 2–3 days, why were we again caught distracted?

So, the difference here is that we resist ourselves. If something is going on unevenly, we don't try to make ourselves flexible with that; on the contrary, we get frustrated, and to get some dopamine, we stick on social networking sites. So, over and over, the above-mentioned "CYCLE OF FRUSTRATION" is repeating itself. But who is the real culprit behind all this? Social networking sites, our brain, or sudden situations. Yet we are unaware of the real culprit behind all this?

The answer to this leading interrogation is "WE OURSELVES." We are the hindrance in our journey; only ourselves can be blamed for this. Why do we get attracted to social media? It's about us. Apparently, to add zeal and get dopamine get attracted by your goals.

Then, concluding it in a simple way, we can say it as a "CYCLE OF FRUSTRATION AND WE."

The creator and operator of this cycle are – we.

Similarly, we can resist as well.

CHAPTER FOURTEEN

OPPORTUNITY & SATISFACTION

" "Don't wait for something because whenever you wait for something, it never comes." You become late in your life to achieve bigger things."

Going through problems is normal. One who masters the skill of handling situations well, that can resolve the issues easily. We all work for our happiness, and everyone is fighting his or her own battle, even though it is not on the ground, as it was earlier. But again, finding the solutions and acting upon them are quite similar.

Daily, we perform some activities that boost our confidence and inspiration and help us become proficient in them. Often, it happens that we wait for opportunities to come so we can act upon them. But it's something that wouldn't be helpful at all. **Waiting for opportunities is a totally an inaccurate approach to our goals.**

"Don't wait or dream for opportunities; create them yourself."

We have limited access to everything, whether it's about time, resources, or chance. And that's why you shouldn't limit yourself. Create every moment like a chance and make every moment count to yourself. Time is flying; at the end, we say, "Where has the time gone?" You should be aware of this. Where is your timing going?

One thing we do is use the word "opportunity" as an excuse. We are like, "When a good chance comes, only then will we be able to do something better."

"You each day is likely the equivalent of the steps on a ladder, those you take daily to reach or achieve success."

It's all up to us what we do. To make yourself a realization daily, ask a question every night to yourself, just before crashing over the bed.

Have I done something satisfactory to make this day countable?

CHAPTER FIFTEEN

COURAGE & FEAR

" "Courage and fear both are opposite, but they share a common character of demolition. Courage can demolish fear and fear can demolish courage." "

Being strong every inch of time, isn't something which can be expected from one. So many troubles are there, it becomes quite impossible condition, to stay strong all the time. Our whole courage seems to be diminished away, in tough times. Our fear and courage both work parallel. To understand it, let's consider a case:

Let's say you are facing off a tough time, it could be any situation, for instance, your company is in huge lose, you got scared from dark, you have fear from height. In these situations, losing strength, being afraid both are common.

If one just thinks to give up, just because being afraid from the condition, this is how our fear can naturally demolish courage and we will lose the streak. On the other hand, if one is going to gather some courage, it is natural that we will not lose. Even if we lose something, learn from it. Don't be hard on yourself. But be a bit strict towards yourself, that's what needed more.

CHAPTER SIXTEEN

PROGRESS DATA

""Indulge a better life and good things after indulging all obstacles and failures.""

Firstly, let's ask two questions to ourselves:

- Who don't want to have good life?
- Who don't want heaven?

In both these cases, we have to struggle.

In the first scenario, we have to face off struggle, have to bond ourselves with some limits i.e., being strict ourselves; have to go through with obstacles.

In the second scenario, if one want to live in heaven, one has to die firstly. So, as a conclusion we can say this, we have to clash with obstacles.

We all are afraid from problems, we have a believe that only we have problems, others are elated but we all need to understand this, **the external appearance can't showcase the internal picture.** To have a broader view of anything, we have to dive deep. So, it's normal to have stress, negative thought processing. To overcome this, we must keep motivating ourselves.

Failures are the one who teach us to be a proficient in anything. Try, try and try in this process, one is going to make mistakes, however these can't be considered as mistakes, what I call it's "PROGRESS DATA." This data will be useful in every inch of time. Whatever the new learning, one has made, put it in the Excel sheet to analyze it in a better way. This will keep you reminding, keep reviewing the progress data. Keep adding on new and updated data, to know own position. How much progression one has made.

Nothing might be new for you, but as standards are constant, we must create difference by applying.

CHAPTER SEVENTEEN

FOCUS

" *"Focus on daydreaming will not give you anything. Instead, consolidating all the powers with a focus on the actions will give you more frequent productivity, and greater success."* "

Who doesn't want to have a successful life? Everyone wants it. Nevertheless, so many things are there, which keep on going. We are fed up with these hurdles. These things make us unpredictable. It tends to lose focus. Our focus is just on sifting through multiple things. We keep on sifting our focus from one thing to other.

As we try to grasp the knowledge of one thing, problems are always there. However, we can't deny this universal fact that, whatever we do, we have to face ups and downs. We can follow these points listed below to retain our focus.

A. Prepare an Excel sheet: Whatever the skill, one is trying to be proficient in that. For this, simply prepare an Excel sheet; this sheet will contain all the data and information you need. For instance, if one is trying to learn a new language, in that case:

- List down the strategy you have decided to learn.
- List down the new vocabulary.
- Write phrases and all other necessary material that you have learned or want to revise.

Above-mentioned points will indirectly help us, to keep motivated to learn new things.

B) Healthy exercises: The exercises would mean physical work to you, although it's not just about physically performing the exercises. These healthy exercises mean to perform some mental exercise. What does it even mean? Whenever we carry out an identical exercise, it also seems to no longer have the interest, and when interest seems to be diminished, naturally the focus tends to be suppressed. Taking the above-mentioned example of learning a language, if one is going to gain an understanding with old techniques, i.e., learning 5 words a day, this really will not work in the long run. It's known to me that only a few can maintain this for long, and only those few will learn; in contrast, we have other lots of things that keep on going, ups and downs. And it becomes hard to maintain. For this, executing mental exercises becomes essential. But what can one pull off?

For this, learning through interactive applications and using technology has become crucial. All applications become attractive due to their user-friendly interfaces. Taking the help of technology in different directions will work. Using physical methods, it will include flashcards, as is obvious, and sticky notes will be useful.

Using different ways to learn and revise is a healthy exercise.

These things will help in retaining the knowledge and the interest will continue to remain focused.

CHAPTER EIGHTEEN

RIGHT DECISION

""If you think that a decision is just a decision, always remember that a single decision, right or wrong, whatever you take, is the consequence of your future.""

Everything we face off we want everything to be sorted; that's what is not constant. In our lives, we believe we only get the chance to decide something a few times, even though it's true to some extent. However, Daily, we get the chance to decide. How?

Let's say you are a student.

On this day, you have a couple of things that want to be done. You have already planned out your day. For instance, like this:

5:00 a.m.: wake up
5:30-6:00 a.m.: Exercises
6:00–9:00 a.m.: Study session – 1
Break
11:00 a.m.-11:00 p.m.: Study session No. 2
3:00-5:00 p.m.: Study session – 3
7:00–9:00 p.m.: Study session – 4

10:00–11:00 p.m.: Night rituals

11:00 p.m.: crashing over the bed

This is the proper planning you have done. In contrast,

The beginning of your day wasn't good. You have faced many sudden situations that were not expected. Now, when unexpected situations occur, we all become frustrated with the day. Why does everything bad happen to me?

In this situation, decisions play a crucial role. Say your half of the day got wasted; the frustration level is already at its peak. What would you do? Again, let's use the help of two case scenarios:

Case 1: Let the day waste.

Case-2: Do the work, even if it's half or even less than that.

Which will you choose?

CASE – 2 ....??

However, at that moment, the majority doesn't take a decision; that's the mistake.

People think, "Okay, my day got ruined, but I will not let my other days get spoiled like this one." For this one, I'm going to plan again.

If one is going to take a decision, I wouldn't let external forces break my confidence or ruin my day. Apparently, even if one has done a little, that will bring real happiness.

"One stubborn decision can change your whole life. Taking it at the right time is the major thing that always matters."

CHAPTER NINETEEN

ENJOYABLE MOMENTS

> *"A moment sometimes becomes a memory forever, so always insist on enjoying every moment."*

Only we know how hard our lives are. What people think about us isn't a good idea. We shouldn't think this about ourselves. We need to enjoy the moments; every single day showcases different views. And these views give us various emotions. Some parts of the day might be filled with happy emotions, and some parts of the day might insist that we feel sad. It could be either a depressed or angry state. We all suffer from this; however, we don't need to skip this thought, that we must reap the benefit during a happy state.

Although there are exceptional cases, if one comes under the weather in this kind of situation, no one will be able to feel good, no matter how much we insist.

In case you are a student:

You have secured a lower score; here, you don't need to overstress in this regard. You must do bit relax, find the wrong question, go through them again, and in case you don't get it, ask the tutor.

In case you are a working professional:

Having stuff to be done, a heavy workload, stress, and anxiety are common emotions. Not getting a desirable position. It happens, however, if one is going to take it on the high node. It wouldn't work in the right manner.

So, this becomes crucial here; one needs to enjoy the moments while performing the tasks by showing interest in them.

Be mindful of...

"What we like, we always want to do for whole of the day."

"In contrast, what we don't like, we even don't want to give a look at that."

That's why it's necessary to enjoy the moments of life, it's our life and we need to cheer up ourselves.

- Try to take less stress of unexpected situations.
- Learn to make ourselves happy.

CHAPTER TWENTY

TODAY & MANIFESTATION

"*"Fight daily with yourself not to fight for a better life in the future."*"

Let's consider two statements:

STATEMENT-1:

We all have a belief that when we will be at that stage of our lives, we will execute this plan or perform this task.

And we put it in the journal.

This is what is meant by "MANIFESTATION."

Is this (MANIFESTATION) true?

STATEMENT-2:

Manifestation:

In simple words, something theoretical became real.

How are these two above-mentioned statements related to each other?

We have some thoughts regarding our plan, and we try to do some research on that topic. The next step we perform is to write down the strategy, either using pen and paper or digitally. This is the theory; these are the actions that we will perform; this is the process, and at last, we have made it real.

Because the theoretical planning become true.

Now, both statements are related to each other. Theoretical planning one have made, it has become real. And manifestation means theoretical planning or data becomes true.

However, what's the conclusion?

This will be cleared at the end.

Now, it's about manifestation. ***Does manifestation really become true?***

Does everything become true just by putting in journal? Just what, we were calling was: Manifestation.

Let's say one got a chance to ask the question to the universe.

If one is going to ask this question to the universe, what will the universe say about this?

So, let's say we have written down all our manifestations in our journal.

Let's ask this question to the universe:

- When will I be able to complete this task?
- When will I get these marks?
- When will my company have this much (as per your wish) in net worth?

The universe will answer these questions after asking us one question.

"What have you done to accomplish this task?"

What will you answer?

Our answer is, umm, universe. I have written down everything in my journal, and that's all.

Now, how can manifestation become true? To make them true, we must perform actions; we must execute the plans.

Can we say now that manifestations have come true? The straightforward answer for this is that when the needed actions are put on that plan, why not it becomes true?

Daily, we must perform the action plan; continuity in the process is much needed. It's better to fight now than wait until later.

CHAPTER TWENTY-ONE

OUR RECORD

""Always determine some goals on a regular basis. The regular tracking helps enrich us and helps in our self-development.""

Let us begin by six questions.

- What are your goals?
- Why have you chosen that goal?
- What is special about you?
- What are you doing to accomplish that goal?
- How do you keep yourself motivated?

One last question: **how do you review yourself?**
Why am I asking these questions?
I'm asking you to ask yourself these questions.
We start multitudinous with lots of zeal, but without doubt, after some days, the energy peak starts falling. The graph starts showing the downfall.

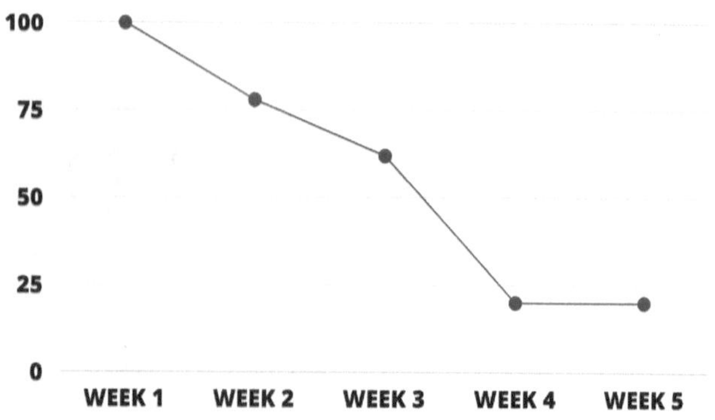

FIGURE - 4 ZEAL GRAPH

As in the above graph, it is visible that we try with diligence, but gradually it starts to diminish. To maintain this graph, it becomes crucial that we continue to track ourselves.

Here are some of the tips to be followed to remain trackable:

A) Understand the work: One must understand the action plan for a particular goal.

B) Working—Putting efforts into the work.

C) EXCEL: Why do I always say to have an Excel sheet? This runs an important cycle, and if one is not able to go for Excel, there are multiple ways to remain tracked. Google Sheets are also a good option. One has to just write down the information, do some settings, set reminders, and that's all. Else, everything will be managed by Excel or Google. We just need to put, what we have done and what we want to do. The personalized experience of anything is much needed. As we can't rely on anything just by listening, we

first want to experience it.
"Tracking is the chief factor in self-development."

CHAPTER TWENTY-TWO

IMGINATION OF SECONDS

""Everyone is obsessed with material things; affection towards material things is OKAY, but we all have one thing we should be mindful of, and that is "NOW." [present time]"

We all have ambitions; no one is there who does not want to fulfil his or her ambitions. Imagine that when I'm at that position, I'll be doing this, this, and that. These kinds of thoughts are not rare. However, we are all afraid to take part in difficult levels. Something we got easily; will we value it? The worth of anything matters.

Considering a case: You are a content creator, you have a good number of followers, people know you, and they know you through your work.

Let's say you are a content creator in the field of "life coaching" and you create videos on life lessons.

You have done a good number of seminars; now a college or an institute is offering you some X amount to give an offline session.

The scenario here is that they are offering you less than you are worth. So, in this case, one needs to be mindful of the fact that worth matters.

Similarly, the value of time DOES matter.

Imagining the accomplishment of goals isn't a wrong thing; in contrast, thinking on and on is the worst. What I call it is an "IMAGINATION OF SECONDS."

This thing that one is doing and keeping on thinking about the moments the goal accomplishment moments is just for seconds. What will remain are "NOW ACTIONS, BETTER FUTURE."

One needs to learn the reality of life. Only this will give you real motivation.

"Present time" is crucial.

CHAPTER TWENTY-THREE

KNOWLEDGE OF ROAD-MAP

" "Going through with a roadmap for a particular thing is always better than going to be messed up; as said earlier, we are our own obstacles. "

Let's consider two cases:

Case 1: Learning Skills

So, if one wants to learn a new skill—either language or programming language, dancing, painting, content -marketing, calligraphy, or any other skill. What will one be doing to accomplish the goal?

- Research

- Plan

- Action

But here, one leaves out some points, that are not negligible.

A. Interest – Why do I emphasise interest all the time? This is what makes us consistent throughout the journey of learning. Consider, you have interest in another field, but due to some unavoidable circumstances, you have chosen another field without having any interest in it. Now, it becomes a crucial factor here.

Even if one doesn't like the job, in contrast of, one starts taking interest, one can achieve more success in that field as well.

B) RESEARCH – Now, performing the research task is beneficial, when we get to know more about a particular thing, our curiosity gradually increases.

C) MAPPING – Again, the crucial factor is there: "MAPPING." Plot out important topics. For example, if one is learning a new language, there are some important topics that can't be ignored.

D) Constant Sources – This the chief factor. The sources should be definite.

One can't be like this.

Day -1: YouTube

Day 2: Vocabulary from social media sites

Day-3: Break

Day-4: Google

Day-5 – It was spent in searching for sources again, and the whole day was gone in that.

This is the thing one should keep off.

No one wants to mess up, which is why definite sources are important.

D) To be Consistent

E) Completion

"Completion is always long way tougher than starting."

Case 2: You want to do Start Up

What will one do? Knowing a bit like a piece of cake, is it sufficient to grow in 1 or 1.5 years?

It takes many years to reach a position where your company doesn't need an introduction. However, to grow in 1 or 1.5 years at top-notch levels. The necessary knowledge matters.

A plan can be changed to grow more; however, doing everything without prerequisite knowledge is nothing.

It's okay to make mistakes; nevertheless, making mistakes without prescriptive knowledge isn't a fruitful thing.

The road map is much-needed knowledge.

"The roadmap is just like the art of knowledge."

When one doesn't know how to plot a map for itself, knowledge of that field is needed.

Without knowledge, doing anything is the biggest mistake.

CHAPTER TWENTY-FOUR

COMPETE WITH COMPLETION

" "To get a better and happier life. Remember to always start now, whenever you realize it."

"Start with whatever you have; end up with what you want to learn."

Complete and compete these both statements. One must explain and prove themselves. If one has started something, it should be completed. However, it doesn't seem to get completed when one's procrastination is there. There are not any magical pills through which one can resist the distractions.

Our day-to-day activities get affected when we always give ourselves the excuses of procrastinating. The journey of something, which started earlier or will be starting, will take a long time to complete. For completion, it's known to us that we should keep off all the distractions, but nevertheless, we're all kind of addicted to this. Every consequence is known to us. However, getting over the distractions is not an easy task.

It's our life; no one is here to prove himself or herself to another one.

That's why it's important that we all prove ourselves to ourselves.

We need to understand this thing:

- *Our topmost competition is completion.*
- *Represent yourself as a candidate.*
- The realization is again important.
- To do so, keep reminding yourself.
- Either use digital ways or paste sticky notes all over the walls.

Whatever one has started should be completed. This is just the kind of competition one needs to achieve.

CHAPTER TWENTY-FIVE

CONCEPT OF ATTRACTION

> *"Everyone can create their own thinking, but only a few people in this universe make their thinking true."*

We have an abundance of thoughts springing in our mind. We believe this is something we want. However, every single thought remains constant as our thinking, until the, we take steps. Whatever one wants to achieve in his or her life, it's important that we take forward steps towards that. One needs to be mindful of the concept of attraction here.

Whatever we think, we believe it's our manifestation. And manifestations are there to be completed. But do they get completed just by repeatedly thinking about them or journaling about them? Obviously, the answer is "NO." This is the wrong approach to the attraction concept.

The universe will only show us the way.

But what's the concept of attraction?

Do you think there are no binding rules for this?

Fundamentally, there are binding rules for this.

RULES:

- The steps *(ACTIONS)* one is going to take for upliftment.
- The perseverance towards the work.
- Apparently, the repeated word "COMPELETION."

This is the concept, and these are the rules of the "CONCEPT OF ATTRACTION."

Now there is a question that arises: Which is the thing that works as a hindrance?

THE TIME WHEN:

"Our thinking becomes much greater than our execution."

Our performed actions will help to make things true.

CHAPTER TWENTY-SIX

PERMISSION OF QUIT

""Permission is something we ask someone for when we are performing or not performing any task, but when we get exhausted by any task, do we ask for or take permission from ourselves to stop any task?""

Think

When we start any task, it's the best experience we have had. Although it's a wrong statement that only best experience is beginning, then, what is the best experience?

"WHOLE JOURNEY"

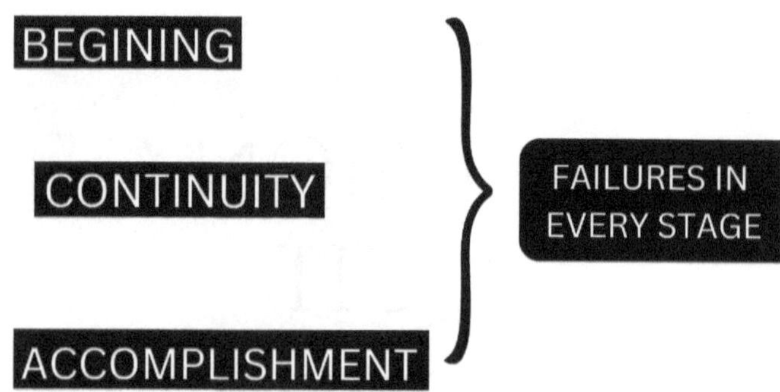

FIGURE – 5

As shown in the above figure, every single stage gives us a good learning experience; it is up to us how we feel, either getting depressed or feel elated over learning something new.

What we need to feel for the victory is "*COMPLETION.*" This is the exact moment to say, it is our victory. We all are not just for diminutive things. Something big we want and have to achieve on our own. *We need to make ourselves capable of that.* The question that might arise in one's brain is, "*How can I say this, that one need to make capable?*" One is not sufficiently capable of doing so. It's not that one doesn't have the skills. **This capability is about "consistency."**

This is hard to maintain all the time. That's the quality one needs to develop.

Whenever we got exhausted by working, without doubt, we just had one thought:

Let's just pause,

and then this pause gives us another thought of:

"Let's just quit!"

In contrast of, we don't give up on our bad habits. For example

- Junk food
- Not having proper sleep
- Not performing exercises

We don't say, "I need to make them correct." They are ongoing. **Then why don't we adopt the habit of consistency if it is good for us?**

We don't want to quit, but without asking ourselves first, we just quit.

This habit of ourselves, we need to change.

CHAPTER TWENTY-SEVEN

WE

" "By hating yourself,
You will lose yourself.
By loving yourself,
You will be loved by everyone." "

What we want for ourselves is not constant. It varies just like a student's grade list or a graph of business growth. Sometimes, we do not exactly know what kind of emotions we are going through. No-one experiences just one kind of emotion for the whole day. Our emotions are quite simply comparable with a business progress data graph. BUT HOW?

Is this true?

Exactly not, but it is comparable.

We can say this: the graph of a company's progress is not constant. Similarly, the emotions are not constant at all.

Something being constant in practical life, which we are all experiencing, is not possible.

Nevertheless, the emotion of frustration is often unknown. While experiencing different kinds of situations, we experience different emotions. When we all go through with this, we forget one emotion to feel. That is *"making a soft corner for ourselves."*

When we fail to accomplish the goals, when we experience the demotivated situation while in the low energy zone, we all feel hate. Our hate rate increases because we believe, "I am not capable of anything."

That's why it's important that we love ourselves.

Whatsoever we want, it is for our happiness, we are doing it for our satisfaction.

We should work for our happiness.

CHAPTER TWENTY-EIGHT

CONFRONTING

""Confront the reality of life, that to get something in life, we have to confront society, and to confront society, we have to confront ourselves.""

We are the brainstormers. It is always our goal to do something unique. Several different ideas keep striking in our minds. However, before its completion, we try to quit it. People mostly think about what society will say. Society will not say a word. It's us; we make it complex.

What is the reason behind the uncompleted task?

To save ourselves from the situations, we can state multiple reasons, or what we can say as excuses.

- I am not able to control my procrastination.
- Time management is difficult.
- Not able to focus for long periods of time.
- What will society say?
- I can't get over my addiction to mobile phones.

So many repetitive excuses we can give to ourselves to just stay far away from difficult situations.

So, these excuses are formed by us; we are the only ones who are the producers of these tantrums. The creators can make the change as per requirements.

Although, we are not taking steps in the right direction. *Putting all the efforts into not performing the excused action will be literally helpful.* So, the main reason is "WE OURSELVES."

When we will be putting all the efforts in the right direction, in enhancing ourselves, stop being the production house of excuses. We will literally win. Sometimes, the anonymous conditions occur, which might not seem to be controllable. Nevertheless, we need to exceed them as well. We need to prepare ourselves for the unknown situations.

CHAPTER TWENTY-NINE

OUR DECISION

""We prefer easy paths to success, but success is already a difficult path, so shortcuts always add more troubles in the journey.""

We all like to have the simplest pathway for anything. No matter what. We are all aware that nothing is easily obtained. Yet, we try to do so. If something is simple and approachable, because it does not worth much. But this statement does not mean, everything which is available free of cost, it's useless. What benefits us, we need to figure out by own.

Similarly, if something is difficult to approach, it will be worth a lot as well. But does it have to be something expensive? Only if it is of high quality. Here, it's not about the cost or quality of the material. The point that is highlighted here is to fight for the good things. The struggle itself is something worthwhile. It will teach us to be strong in the hard times. Who gives us the hard time?

Who is responsible for our hard times?
It is "US."
How do I directly state this statement?

In the beginning of the journey, our creator helps us to grow by checking our abilities. Our creator gave us the difficulties to make us strong enough for other situations. That's the time to rebuild ourselves. When we fail to do so, we fail to build up ourselves.

Now, it is about "us." We have changed the rules of creator. Now, it is our turn to face the difficulties. And these difficult times are far more difficult than we could have imagined.

As a result, we can say that this is us. We have chosen hard times for ourselves.

And these hard times give the server mental pain as well.

LIFE CHANGING MOMENTS

> *"Don't be disappointed if you miss out on an opportunity in your life; life must have good plans for you, but only if you work hard to find another one."*

"It's hard to have good opportunities in life."

Is this statement true?

Well, it's a partially true statement, but how? Let's take a deep dive into this:

Everyone gets good opportunities, and those opportunities are considered the "LIFE CHANGING MOMENTS."

However, do the good chances that one receives represent life-changing moments? Without a doubt, "NO." We all get a day with 24 hours, from which 9-10 hours can be easily eliminated.

Like, in sleeping – 6-7 hours

In traveling – 1-2 hours

In morning habits – 1-2 hours

Do we need to focus on those which are fixed 9-10 hours that are easily gone, or do we need to pay attention to the other remaining hours?

So, yes, we must concentrate our efforts on the remaining ones in order to maximize their productivity. And yes, we can try to make changes to get something out of those hours as well.

From the above, one thing is clear:

We get an opportunity every day.

If once a chance gets missed, then *Are these daily opportunities not enough?*

The daily steps will provide us the opportunity.

Now, in the conclusion, another thing can be stated:

Life-changing moments are those that occur once, twice, or more than once, and they occur daily.

CHAPTER THIRTY-ONE

REFILL OR REPLACEMENT

"Refill and replacement are widely used; whenever people get bored, they choose to replace, but refill is only chosen by a few. Those few are successful."

To achieve something, we need to work for it. When we get exhausted from working, we try to think about other options.

We believe, "If I am going to choose another field, it will be easier to achieve."

Although this is true according to our mind's psychology, but it is difficult to achieve in practice. Nothing is easy to crack.

If someone claims that studying commerce or humanities is simple. The students belonging to that category are not very capable of doing anything. That's the point that needs changing. Whatever a person's profession or field is. Every course is demanding.

EVERY FIELD DEMANDS SKILLS AND PERFECTIONISM.

The knowledge, the skills, and the practical or experimental view of anything are much needed.

By looking at the numerous online resources like by watching videos none of us can drive a car on the first try. Nobody can learn to play the guitar or violin by simply watching. The practical performance of the tasks is crucial.

As a result, following the replacement is not a good idea. Rather than replacing, replenish knowledge within yourself so that you are not replaced by your position.

Add zeal and refill the needs for a beautiful journey.

CHAPTER THIRTY-TWO

BOOST-UP

""A small kick can sometimes make a big difference in our lives, so be inspired by these kicks to have all the glory in the future.""

To enjoy the glory, we are bound by the rules. Do we have to follow any rules in order to enjoy our lives?

We shouldn't be, however, directly or indirectly we do, but what are those rules? Is everyone among us following those rules?

Rule 1: Limiting Ourselves

We all exaggerate situations; we believe that any problem is the most terrifying condition we have ever faced in our lives. We limit ourselves to not feeling elated while experiencing these conditions. We need to give ourselves a boost and remember to be happy.

RULE-2: -

Let's start it with an understanding of an example:

Consider yourself a small businessman who runs a small business. Consider the following occupations as well: tailor, barber, cordwainer, and plumber.

The business is at a moderate level of being survivable. One wants to upgrade this to a higher level as a startup. Is it possible to ameliorate it as a startup?

There are different opinions about this statement. Nevertheless

"We can do what we want."

As the most preferred cordwainer are BATA, ADDIDAS and NIKE.

Those who wish to do it as a start-up can do so at a higher level as well. What we want is to give a boost all the time to ourselves.

In a certain state, the unpredictability of our lives resists us. We all need to inspire ourselves to be happy and achieve glory, and to get inspired, we need to elevate ourselves.

CHAPTER THIRTY-THREE

SUKHMAN 1-8 DAY RULE

""Beginning a new journey is always difficult; however, there are only two possible outcomes: 'the best or the worst.' But believe in the process; it will teach something.""

Whatever process one is going through, it becomes hard to accomplish. However, it's true to some extent. Nevertheless, we're all aware of a few things: if something has begun, it should end; if something has begun but has not been completed by the deadline, it will undoubtedly increase anxiety. The two-case scenario is helpful to use here.

Case-1: - If a student was given an assignment that did not have a deadline, they were told to finish it by the end of the month. It is a non-emergency situation.

CASE-2: - On the contrary, students were asked to complete the assignment in the next 5 days. That's the deadline, from now until the time the work is not done. The level of anxiety will remain high.

What's the conclusion, then?

Is it so, that, there is always a deadline needed to complete any task? It's partially a good way to complete the task. Why?

By all means, we all know, there are always some anonymous conditions. Then, what should I do to complete the task? Let us examine the Sukhman 1- 8-Day Rule. WHAT EXACTLY IS THAT RULE STATES? If we have a long or short task. It applies in both cases. The duration is adjustable according to the work period. For example, if one is learning a language, days can be considered as months; similarly, in any other case.

Sukhman 1–8 Days Rule:

Day 1: 1% of work

10% of work in 8 days

On the 12th day, 15% of the work is completed.

In 18 days, 30% of the work is completed.

In 22 days, half of the work is completed.

70% of the work is completed in 30 days.

In 47 days, 85-90% of the work is completed.

On the 60th day, work is completed.

In the above rule, how does one do 10% of the work if it started with only 1%? That's the major point. It is the development of a habit. It is difficult to maintain consistency once one has begun working. If you do that work on a regular basis, the work will be done even before the deadline. It is best to complete the work in 8 days to have a good amount of 10% completed. The worst-case scenario is not doing even 1% on the eighth day.

"It is the development of interest in the work and the development of a new habit of being consistent."

CHAPTER THIRTY-FOUR

UNPLANNED DAYS

""There is a great probability of failure due to unplanned things, but trust, sometimes unplanned days give much fruitful results. So, believe in the pathway and enjoy the journey.""

We need to face many situations. We all got exhausted from them. But again, believing in the fact that good things take time to happen, we always need to conjugate ourselves to pursue the same thing without fail. **However, it's the pathway itself, which is nothing without the difficult times.**

If an entrepreneur fails in his or her startup, is he not able to do business? The answer to this is "no." Then what's the reason behind a failure Start-up?

The foremost thing is that it's not all about the start-up, if anyone fails to perform better in something. That one is not enough for that. That's an entirely wrong statement. There can be multiple reasons for that as well.

- Having less knowledge about the field.
- Putting the wrong strategies all the time.
- Communication credibility.
- Didn't reach the target audience.

Other multiple reasons can also be mentioned. However, the point to be highlighted is that failing for some reasons is not the end of everything. We all need to prepare ourselves all the time. There are multiple start-up owners are there who failed, even though, without losing hope, they have continued their work. The leading examples are Jeff Bezos, Walt Disney, Sir Richard Branson, and Ghazal Alagah, and the list is not limited to a certain number. Nevertheless, the unplanned things are there, which make us demotivated. So, the only thing we need to focus on is not getting stressed out by sudden things. These unplanned days can even be turned into good quality results if we keep working for them.

CHAPTER THIRTY-FIVE

UNIVERSE GIFTS

""Life gives us many gifts, like troubles, problems, or challenges. Let us give a gift to our lives by achieving your desires and giving happiness to ourselves.""

When someone is enjoying an easy life without having any troubles in his or her life. It's definite that one will go through the hard times. On this entire world, no one was there who didn't face any troubles; no one is there who is quite satisfied with their life. However, it's not about the satisfaction; it's about the hard times gifted by the universe. To make us stronger, the universe has gifted us with challenges. To make ourselves capable of something, we must work for it. And while performing those actions, one has to understand the challenges. To know ourselves better, we must overcome challenges.

When a business graph shows some increment, it definitely has to confront strenuous situations, and just to overcome and take a rank in the high position, it's crucial to deal with arduous competition.

During that time, one support is always much needed, and that is "OUR SUPPORT." We are supposed to be leaving ourselves in the middle of the river and go ghost. That's the mistake: we always need to have a "self-talk." Having frequent self-talk is even another beneficial way. What's the benefit of that?

- We got to know ourselves better.
- Our strengths become clear to us.
- We all got familiar with our weaknesses.
- Help us to understand situations better.

On account of this, can we say self-talk is needed? Saying this isn't wrong, however, it's partially true. Our hard work is again an important factor.

Another important thing is:

One of the best gifts we can give ourselves is overcoming all the challenges and continuing to take advantage of the daily opportunities. We all need to work for that as well.

CHAPTER THIRTY-SIX

PROPERTY OF OIL

"Water is colorless, but when it is mixed with anything, it becomes soluble, but when oil is mixed with water, it becomes insoluble. Only like that, adopt the property of oil."

We all have a lot of problems. There is always a booster needed for us to get over them. We all get to meet up with many different people, and in this technological age, we are connected worldwide. We all like having some good friends around all the time to be our backbone. However, there is something to be mentioned here: there are a few people who leave us in between. And we got stressed with that.

Multiple questions arise in one's mind.

- Why did that one does this to me?
- Am I not good?
- Why do all these things happen to me?

Nevertheless, why am I even saying these questions? Is it about not having friends?

Well, no, it's not about having friends. It's about how if someone gets disheartened by these situations, that person needs to overcome them. We will all meet many people. But keep thinking about that one person, who isn't worth you. It's not the right idea.

We don't need to make ourselves like water to get dissolved in everything. To excel, we need to adopt the properties of oil.

Pushing ourselves into a hard phase isn't a good way to grow.

CHAPTER THIRTY-SEVEN

FLAME OF PERTINACIOUS

"Everyone has a light inside them that enables them to perform anything. Only one thing is required, and that is FLAME OF PERTINACIOUS."

We all come across the idea of:

To achieve high, we must do big.

However, it's known to us that we can't build an empire in 2-3 months.

To achieve big things, we need to take steps, even if they are small ones. We are aware of the behaviour of our journey and that we need to face off hassles. *The thing that is approachable isn't a thing of much zeal.*

All the ideas that spring into our minds, we don't execute properly. The idea of being a businessman is good. However, one doesn't know how to be a businessman. Knowledge is again an important factor here. One wants to be either a dancer, a painter, a choreographer, a photographer, or anything else. There are multiple things there; there is a long list of passions. What we want to be, we are all determined to be. What's the obstacle, then? *"IT IS US"* we don't push our limits. We are our own worst enemy. We just need a flame of pertinacious here. Nevertheless, what's the role of being a PERTINACIOUS?

Let's take a deep dive into this:

- What we want to be, it is already determined.

If not,

- Then, all one has to do is search. No one can tell us what we want to be. People can guide us, nevertheless we must follow the path, and must find what we want.

If one is already on the journey to achieve the destination, one should keep on exploring. Once one gets paused for a while, the whole attentiveness will be suppressed for a while. Exactly, no one wants this thing to happen, for this keep on moving.

If one got paused for a while, the one will have to wait for long, as a universal rule, the present time will not come again.

One must keep on lighting the flame.

"The undivided attention elevates the motivation, and the obstinacy towards the goal keeps the work continuing."

This is the time to follow this obstinate.

CHAPTER THIRTY-EIGHT

A BILLIONAIRE

" "Continuous hard work and unstoppable moves make you an unstoppable and successful person." "

Whatever the definition of life is, but one thing is constant, it's all about the struggles; no one knows what is going on in others' lives.

Then there is no need to be so hard on ourselves to achieve something. There must be an attitude of achieving something but pushing in the depression zone isn't the best way at all. We are all supposed to be billionaires; however, only 0.08% of people are billionaires not even 1%. This Is what Statics state.

"Why,"

It is the only question that arises.

However, the only answer to this question can't be suggested. Nevertheless, there are three points that can be highlighted to be the billionaires.

- Knowledge

The most crucial factor of being a successful person is knowledge. We all know that to be a successful person, it is not a game of 1-2 years; if one wants that, there is no even need of an introduction.

- Continuous work

This is something that is needed all the time. To show persistence towards the work or the goals.

- Connections

Being connected with the people of your own field is important. The learning can be made easy. The connections play crucial role in gaining knowledge.

CHAPTER THIRTY-NINE

MANAGEMENT

" "Differences have always been part of our lives. Like if we are busy instead of that, we think we are productive." "

Being busy and being productive are entirely different things. Is it true to state that statement?

We all want to get the most out of our days. The more we ripe, the more it elevates us. However, it's not that we're all going to have productive days all the time.

Consider yourself an entrepreneur who has started coaching or consulting. The peak substitutes. To maintain it all the time isn't possible. One thing that is important to mention is:

"The less work we have,

More we distract."

To prove the statement,

Let's say one wants to be a content creator.

In the new business, one wants to scale up; for this, one needs to upgrade himself or herself. Upgradation is the necessity of life. No matter what the field is, for upgrading ourselves, we have to put extra time and effort. Without that, it wouldn't be possible.

Now, the content creators have a lot of stuff to manage. Managing one's own learning, uploading content, and other so many things are there that need to be managed. Now, one will be able to manage more in less time. Because it's already known to that person that, *I have so much stuff to be done, now I need to handle everything in a better and more suitable manner. The fewer distractions there will be, the better results will generate.*

At the end, it's not incorrect to say this:

<u>"The more work we have,</u>

<u>It's easy to manage."</u>

That's why we need to keep ourselves busy, however productively.

THOUGHTS AUTHORITY

"You are responsible for the good and bad consequences of your life. It is dependent on your daily attitude."

No matter what the task is, we all perform it on a daily basis. It's just like a record. One thing is clear:

How we treat our days determines how our lives will treat us in the future. Our day-to-day activities are included in our progress report. All that we want requires action. No one is there for us to help us out, to be productive, to progress us. To motivate us, to not be stressed; Our thoughts should inspire us to work. Our thoughts play a very important role. We can inspire ourselves and demotivate ourselves with our thoughts. How?

If we are determined to achieve our goal, we say to ourselves, "This is something I want to accomplish." Being determined for the work, our thoughts are helping us to not be distracted. If we say, "This is something I want to accomplish," with this we add another thought that is:

"It's okay; I have some time; I can do it later on." Then, *our brain will automate like that; okay, you have plenty of time.*

Brain commands—I want dopamine, to get dopamine-

- The easiest way to get distracted by social media sites.

However, it does not mean that, social media sites are bad for us. How we use, it matters. Social media sites are good for learning, posting the work online, searching and following the people of own field help us to learn more.

Another dominant point is:

- "It's useless to blame someone for our own future; because life is what we make."

It's all up to us; putting castigation on others is worthless.

"Never give the authority of your life to others for decisions."

What we want is best known to ourselves. There is not any other person who knows us in depth. *That's why our life is our priority, and it is our duty to make ourselves happy and successful.*

CHAPTER FORTY-ONE

ANALOGOUS CHARACTERS

" "For the person who practices for anything, everything is easy for him/her. As easy as ABC." "

Whatever we want, we need to put in unbeatable practice and hard work, including smart work.

"The person becomes proficient when he or she practices for it." AT A STRETCH

We all know that to be successful, we need to be consistent. Why do I mention the words knowledge, consistency, hard work, and practice over and over? Because these are the terms that will make us proficient in our field. We all got frustrated listening to these terms. Because these terms are so common among us. We all want something new to hear. What we can do is change the names of these terms.

Hard-work – Tough grinding
Practice – Implementing
Consistency – Regularity

The modifications can be made; however, the function is again similar. It can't be changed. We can add on some modifications to this. Like adding some creative ways to perform any activity.

"Shifting your place is quite difficult; shifting our minds to the right path leads to success."

We need to shift our brains to not follow the excuses like:

- I am not able to focus properly.
- I am not able to maintain consistency.
- I am not able to finish.

The commonly used terms and the modified terms are analogous; they have the same function, but their names got changed.

To be successful, we first need to stop making excuses. After that, we need to use the analogous characters.

In simple words:

Analogous characters are those which perform same function, however the terminologies changed.

CHAPTER FORTY-TWO

RESTRICTIONS

""Clashing your own decisions will help you get the best of it.""

All we need is a successful life. Having a luxurious life is our dream. The difference we need to create is to change this dream into a goal. There are so many plans we made to upgrade our skills, and these skills are helpful to us to upgrade our lives.

Nevertheless, we can't enhance ourselves in just 1 or 2 days. Giving ourselves challenges is the unique way we can be consistent with our work.

We can put a challenge in front of us that, like

"I want to learn this particular thing in 25 days."

For example,

Learning a language is not possible in 25 days or some 50–60-day challenge.

The highlighting point here is that, to start and when it gets started, it is supposed to be a short (20–25 day) challenge. The short challenge for language learning can be like this:

- Learning some X amount of vocabulary in 1520 days.
- Completing grammar rules in some other X number of days. challenge will generate more interest, and it will become our habit. And of course, as we know, habits are not easily faded away.

"Gradually, we can grow, but instant growth might not be possible in a few days." Then always take gradual steps, and success will be yours.

There are multiple things we want to accomplish; however, focusing is the biggest hindrance. Multiple things are there to distract us. That's why **focusing is a much-needed factor.**

Being satisfied might be difficult, so just focus on your goals and achieve big. Then there is no need to get satisfied with limitations.

CHAPTER FORTY-THREE

REALIZATION

"The greatest day in every person's life is that when a person begins to start self-realization."

What we want is only known to all of us. However, some people don't know.

- What do they want?
- What do they want to become?
- What is the passion they want to follow?

It's not easy to get the answers; we need to try out so many things.

People can guide us about the different job options. We can get to know about the different job options; nevertheless, what's best for us is known to us.

We need to keep exposing ourselves to various fields. Nevertheless, one question remains unanswered, and that is:

HOW DO WE KNOW WHAT IS BEST FOR US?

To get this answer, we need to gain experience. It is not that we need to spend our whole time just to get exposed to various fields.

There are certain points that one should keep in mind to get to know better:

1) KNOWLEDGE: If we want to know, we need to get knowledge about the field. When we have knowledge about a field, we know if it is something we can pursue or not.

2) PRACTICAL EXPERIENCE: Now, it's hard to take out time to experience various fields experimentally. But by putting in some extra time and effort, we can get to know better.

3) ANALYSIS: It's time to know what's better. Now that one has the knowledge and the practical analysis, it's easier to get the answer.

That's the best moment, when one knows what's best for himself or herself.

CHAPTER FORTY-FOUR

PRESENT

""We don't have any control over our past; however, our future will be better if we ensure that our present actions are good enough.""

It is known to all of us that:

"OUR REALITY IS OUR PRESENT."

Whatever happened in the past is in the past, including any mistakes we have made in the last few years, months, or even days. All the problems are literally infeasible. If we procrastinated, didn't manage our time, and didn't motivate ourselves to be focused on the goals, it's our fault; we didn't realise at that moment, that this is something that I am doing wrong.

Even though it's known to us,

Yet we do so.

This automatically generates the stress and we:

KEEP DEALING WITH STRESS; AND IT IS A WHOLE MESS THAT WE WILL CREATE.

It's time to give up on the stress and try to live in the present.

Now, if it's known to us that working on the present is something that we need to keep on trying.

But, we believe, 'I don't know how to start.'.

"Playing the truth or dare game with ourselves is much better than seeking answers to our lives from others."

This is something we need to do.

CHAPTER FORTY-FIVE

SEGMENTS

""Whatever we want to learn, it's important to start; more importantly, continuation is essential; and on top of that, ending is a necessity.""

Only we know:

- At which time we wake up?
- What are the morning rituals we perform?
- How much time we devote to our morning rituals.
- According to our profession, what all we do in daily lives?
- Which is the time slot where we are free to perform our interestbased hobbies.

All things vary for everyone. Whether it is a high school student or a college student. Either it's a freelancer, or a content creator, or a working professional.

Meanwhile, we have different time slots for everything.

If we want to master any skill, we need to put the efforts. Again, it's hard to accomplish this. There are five segments for the accomplishment of any particular thing, which we need to follow without giving up and these are listed as below:

1. STARTING
2. CONTINUITY
3. PENDING STATE
4. CONTINUITY
5. ACCOMPLISHMENT

These five things are present in our day-to-day activities. Beginning with,

1) STARTING: There are two scenarios in which we start a work.

A) ZEAL: When we start something with enthusiasm, it will be easier to complete that work.

B) UNWILLING: Sometimes, unwilling, we begin anything; it doesn't matter if we have interest or not.

2) CONTINUITY PHASE-1: We have started performing tasks for the goal. We are doing it with zeal, and with that, we are gradually losing interest in it. Considering Case 2, where the work was started with unwillingness, interest is being generated.

NOTE: It's not about starting unwillingly; it highlights the interest point.

3) PENDING: The growth was amazing in the first few days. Now, gradually, the growth graph is declining. And then the pending state began. We try to put it on other days. When this begins, goal goes into pause mode.

4) CONTINUITY PHASE 2: If we gather ourselves to complete the task, we tend to be in the continuity phase 2.

However, if someone puts it on pause mode over and over, then, it's hard to get back on the Continuity Phase-2.

5) ACCOMPLISHMENT: When are we supposed to be regular on the continuity phase 2.

We can accomplish the goal. Nevertheless, if we don't move ourselves from the pending state to another segment, it will be forever impossible.

CHAPTER FORTY-SIX

HABITS

" "Habit tracker is the necessity to be trackable." "

Our routines and our habits are interconnected with each other. How do I state this statement so directly?

Before diving into it. We need to go through with one psychological fact about our brain:

When we begin something, we are supposed to do it consistently and we seek rapid growth.

Although it's known to us, that the above fact is not universally accepted.

What we think does not mean it is true; it is assumed to be correct, and it will be accepted by the universe. This is the misconception.

Other thing:

We believe our swift development can be seen upon performing the determined actions.

Is this how our brain thinks?

Well, this is not the way our brain thinks.

"We set a protocol for ourselves that doing some particular tasks would give an instant result." This thinking helps our brain get dopamine more easily. That is the biggest hindrance.

Nowadays, when our brain gets dopamine easily, it believes this is something I need to perform. (Keeping on thinking about the outcomes)

Nevertheless, our brain gets the action command less. That's the reason we feel exhausted when we have to perform the actions.

This routine of "keeping on imagining" becomes our habit. When we feel exhausted from our work, we think to get dopamine, which is not a good path to follow. We need to change this incongruity.

"Craft your ideas to make a creative future."

Our actions should be our routine; **what we do daily becomes our habit.** That's why, to improve our pattern of learning, we need to make a change in our routine.

On the path, we will have to face off the problems; we will get the opportunities in case we lose any chance; we do not need to be so hard on ourselves.

"When you become frustrated with your life, be mindful that you have time; one opportunity is lost, but it's not the end."

CHAPTER FORTY-SEVEN

MORNING RITUALS

""Our future is decided by our morning rituals."*"*

What we do, what we want, what we are doing. Our futuristic goals are decided by us.

The lag is only in our actions. The actions that we perform—do they really determine how we will be in the future?

To understand this, let's understand "THE THEORY OF MORNING RITUALS."

Morning rituals are those actions that we perform only in the morning. Well, "NO."

The theory is not just about morning actions.

- If someone wants to be a good reader, what does one have to do?
- If someone wants to be a healthy and fit person in the future, what does one have to do?

The answer to both questions is "TAKING ACTIONS. It is known to us.

How we execute the work is kind of like this:

- We think
- We plan.
- Taking some small actions.
- Feeling demotivated for a while.
- Putting the books on the shelves.
- Forget.

This is what we do.
To keep the work ongoing:

- We need to make it consistent.
- The consistent work turns into a habit.
- Habits turn into morning rituals.

To clarify the morning rituals in a definition, it can be stated as this:

"Doing the work without missing can be considered the morning ritual."

We perform morning rituals without missing them.

- Reading every day will make us good readers.
- Exercising daily will help us to be healthy and physically fit.
- Meditation will help us to be mentally fit.

Other than our profession, our leisure activities can be fixed in our routine, just like our casual morning routine.

We wake up, have water, do some other routine, listen to a podcast, or do whatever other work we do. We don't want to skip it. So, when our goal becomes our morning ritual, there is no way to skip it.

CHAPTER FORTY-EIGHT

EMOTIONS

""The moment you become livid or sad, that moment you lose your happiness.""

No one on earth wants to be sad. Nevertheless, life is all about going through various emotions. What we are not able to achieve leaves us in an emotional state. Something for which we were ambitious, when we needed to go through with phase, there at some state, we feel it is the end of everything. At that moment, we can't lose our faith. However, it is hard to maintain consistency without losing our faith and courage. But it is crucial. These leading factors are all much tougher, but not impossible.

"Unwind yourself from thinking, which doesn't even play a bit of a role in encouraging you in life; ebullient your life to do something."

We can't let ourselves lose the game just because of some changes in our emotional state. Well, it's not just about the emotional state; they indirectly affect us. To illustrate this, consider:

"One is feeling demotivated."

What's the reason behind feeling demotivated?

It's not specified that—what's the reason behind this?

If one is a student, getting less grades could leave one in a demotivated state.

In the case of a businessman, the low growth of the business can leave him in a demotivated state.

The point here is that experiencing various emotions is part of life. *The main highlight is why we feel demotivated.*

It is because our efforts were less than what was required.

Concluding it in a simple way:

We can say that going through with different in life is fine; however, going through life with depressed emotions is not fine just because of our reduced efforts.

For this:

We always need to be mindful of the question:

"Are our actions enough?"

This question will keep on motivating us to maintain the streak.

CHAPTER FORTY-NINE

COORDINATION

""Learning and understanding are the necessities, but more importantly, coordination is essential to clearing the loopholes of anything, even the smallest things.""

We get depressed over diminutive things. Our lives showcase all the experiences to us. We feel zeal, happiness, high and low phases, and demotivation. Every single thing that life gives us is for us. We all know this fact:

Every experience is for learning.

The psychology of our brain is different every time. We will always achieve what we want. It is not universally acceptable. There are some loopholes in everything. What is needed is learning and understanding. Both words, "learning" and "understanding," work functionally and coordinatingly. It is a necessity that they work together in coordination.

How do they work together? To understand this, let's consider the case of two students:

Student (A)

Student (B)

Both have been preparing for the same competitive exam. The student (A) has been trying to learn. The student is trying to grasp more and more knowledge. But student A is missing understanding. Now,

The student (B) is learning and trying to grasp the knowledge as well; however, the student B is not skipping the other factor of understanding. Without understanding the syllabus, pattern, or way of attempting the exam. A student is not supposed to perform better in the exams. The student B is using both learning and understanding coordinately. Now, it is not wrong to state that learning and understanding should work functionally and coordinately.

The learning and understanding are applicable to the business as well.

CONSTANT & NON-CONSTANT

"Freezing on the single way is not a better way; finding a way to face off is even better; or finding a different pathway to accomplish your goal is best."

We need the motivation to keep on track. Maintaining the consistency for a particular task is difficult. We all are aware about the fact that:

Putting the same efforts isn't a possible way to get different results. We need to change the pattern, strategies by the time passes.

There are two possible categories can be seen to get the results.

1. CONSTANT
2. NON-CONSTANT

Constant – There are some factors which can be added in this category. Considering – Focus, Perservence, Coordination of left and right brain to get work done.

Non-Constant – The factors like, thinking, planning, strategy fall under this category. These are the factors which can be changed accordingly.

The crucial highlight is the results will be produced by using these both categories. The coordination of everything is crucial. Just like, the team spirit and coordination of a team is important to win the match.

However, we think, using just a single category will be helpful. Nevertheless, we do not need to forget the coordination is important.

To illustrate:

A student wants to score better one is using the same strategy (NON-CONSTANT) and having less focus, low consistency. (CONSTANT)

The results will be the same. Now, working with coordination, will improve.

Using Non-Constant, means, changing in planning and using the Constant means, increment in the focus and consistency, will definitely improve the grades. This categorization is not only applicable on the students, but also on everyone by virtue of their profession.

Short Note

"After facing off the hard times, the time comes where we feel, now the time to get relaxed but eventually it is that time where we have to put more thousand times efforts. Life is unpredictable. Let be little prepared for it, atleast your hard work should be the strongest."

Put your thousand percent efforts with happiness.

It's not the ending, it's the beginning.

That is why maintain a bond with the reality of life.

www.ingramcontent.com/pod-product-compliance
Lightning Source LLC
Chambersburg PA
CBHW021228130726
47988CB00002B/872